SUPERSTORM SANDY

by Rachel Bailey

Content Consultant
Dr. J. Marshall Shepherd
Director, Atmospheric Sciences Program
University of Georgia

CORE
LIBRARY

Published by ABDO Publishing Company, PO Box 398166, Minneapolis, MN 55439. Copyright © 2014 by Abdo Consulting Group, Inc. International copyrights reserved in all countries. No part of this book may be reproduced in any form without written permission from the publisher. The Core Library™ is a trademark and logo of ABDO Publishing Company.

Printed in the United States of America,
North Mankato, Minnesota
052013
112013

♻ THIS BOOK CONTAINS AT LEAST 10% RECYCLED MATERIALS.

Editor: Blythe Hurley
Series Designer: Becky Daum

Library of Congress Control Number: 2013932007

Cataloging-in-Publication Data
Bailey, Rachel.
 Superstorm Sandy / Rachel Bailey.
   p. cm. -- (History's greatest disasters)
ISBN 978-1-61783-961-0 (lib. bdg.)
ISBN 978-1-62403-026-0 (pbk.)
Includes bibliographical references and index.
1. Hurricane Sandy, 2012--Juvenile literature. 2. Hurricanes--United States--Juvenile literature.   I. Title.
363.34--dc23

                                        2013932007

Photo Credits: US Air Force, Master Sgt. Mark C. Olsen/AP Images, cover, 1; NOAA/AP Images, 4; Collin Reid/AP Images, 7; National Hurricane Center/AP Images, 10; Time & Life Pictures/Getty Images, 13; Rex Features/AP Images, 18; Jose Luis Magana/AP Images, 20; Mel Evans/AP Images, 22; Toby Talbot/AP Images, 24; Red Line Editorial, 26, 31; The Star-News, Ken Blevins/AP Images, 28; Mike Groll/AP Images, 30, 33, 45; Ramin Talaie/Corbis/AP Images, 36; Craig Ruttle/AP Images, 40

CONTENTS

CHAPTER ONE

SANDY POUNDS THE CARIBBEAN

Dark rain clouds hung over the sea in the southern Caribbean. With its spinning winds still under 39 miles per hour (63 km/h), this storm was only a tropical depression. It was not yet a hurricane. Scientists from the National Hurricane Center (NHC) kept a careful watch on the storm. When its winds strengthened to 40 miles per hour (64 km/h), the NHC named the storm Sandy. Sandy became the

Hurricane Sandy moves north across Cuba as it heads for the United States.

The Saffir-Simpson Scale

The Saffir-Simpson Scale shows wind speeds and the height of water surges during each of the five hurricane categories. The NHC uses this scale to give hurricanes a rank of 1 to 5. Category 1 hurricanes have sustained winds of 74 to 95 miles per hour (119 to 153 km/h). They normally damage power lines, trees, roofs, and siding on houses. A Category 3 or higher hurricane is considered a major hurricane. A Category 5 hurricane has sustained winds of 157 miles per hour (253 km/h) or more. Hurricanes this severe destroy most buildings in their path. They can leave people without power for weeks or even months.

eighteenth tropical storm of the year on October 22, 2012.

Jamaica

It only took Sandy two days to gain energy from the warm Caribbean waters. On October 24, Sandy became a hurricane. It made landfall on Jamaica's southeastern coast. The NHC measured this Category 1 hurricane at wind speeds of 80 miles per hour (129 km/h).

Citizens looked desperately for shelter. Howling winds snapped trees and power lines.

Hurricane Sandy hits Jamaica with heavy rainfall and strong winds.

Thousands of people were left without electricity. Floods and mudslides threatened the island. Many Jamaicans live in shacks. They feared the storm would destroy their homes.

Haiti

While Jamaicans began to clean up, Haitians prepared for the worst. The hurricane's center missed Haiti. But violent storms hit the country on October 24 with 20 inches (51 cm) of rain. Flash floods and mudslides followed.

Many victims fled their homes and took refuge in temporary shelters. Emergency workers were scarce. The government provided little assistance.

Cuba

Sandy hit Cuba early on October 25. With winds over 110 miles per hour (177 km/hr), it had become a Category 3 hurricane. Sandy's powerful winds ripped off roofs and destroyed homes. It uprooted trees and downed power lines.

Sandy knocked out both water and electricity in Santiago de Cuba, Cuba's second-largest city. Sandy was Cuba's most destructive storm since 2005. That year, Hurricane Dennis killed 16 people in Cuba.

Living in Poverty

In January 2010 a massive earthquake struck Haiti. It killed more than 200,000 people. Haiti dealt with tropical storm Isaac in August 2012. This storm caused at least 29 deaths. Haiti has not recovered fully from these disasters. Lack of money is one of the main reasons. Haiti is the poorest country in the Western Hemisphere. Eighty percent of Haitians live in poverty.

The Bahamas

Late in the evening on October 25, Sandy headed north to the Bahamas. The storm's winds died down to speeds of 90 miles per hour (145 km/h). Sandy was now a Category 1 hurricane.

The Bahamas is made up of many small islands. Officials said the greatest damage was on Cat Island. Strong winds smashed trees, cut power lines, and damaged homes there. On Long Island, farmers lost their crops. People there did not have fresh water to drink. Residents of Acklins Island waded through flooded roads. Floodwaters submerged the only school on Ragged Island.

The storm left the Caribbean with a death toll of 70. Fifty-four of those deaths were in Haiti. After leaving the Caribbean, Hurricane Sandy moved toward the United States.

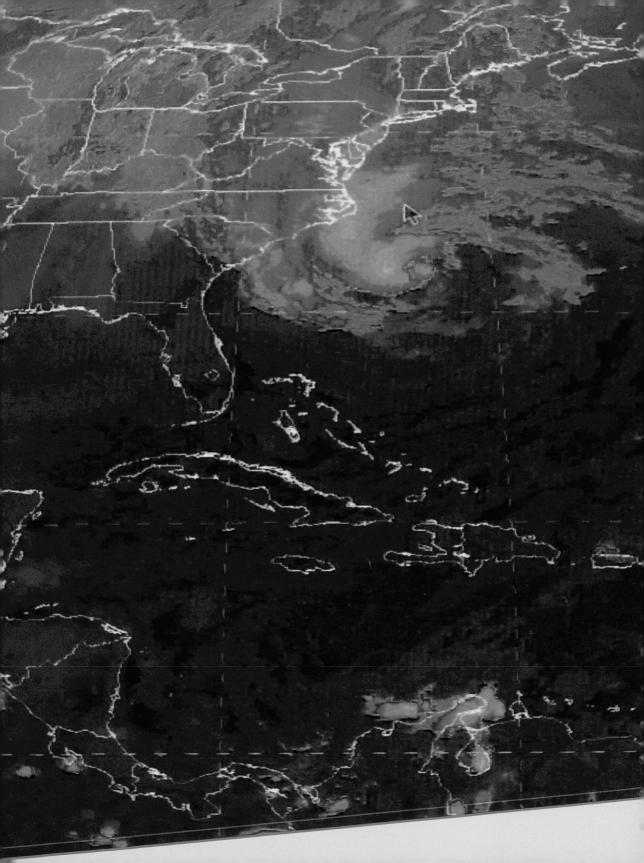

CHAPTER TWO

HURRICANES 101

As Caribbean islanders picked up after Sandy, Americans kept an eye on the hurricane. They knew they were in the path of this swiftly growing storm.

Storms like Sandy are known generally as tropical cyclones. A tropical cyclone is a rotating cloud system. These systems form over tropical waters.

This satellite image from the National Hurricane Center shows Hurricane Sandy barreling into the East Coast of the United States.

In the northwestern Pacific, tropical cyclones are called typhoons. In the Indian Ocean and South Pacific, they are called cyclones. In the Atlantic Ocean, Eastern Pacific, Caribbean Sea, and Gulf of Mexico, tropical cyclones are called hurricanes. The Atlantic hurricane season generally lasts from June 1 to November 30 each year.

Hurricane Formation

Hurricanes are huge storms with heavy rains and powerful winds. They usually form over warm ocean waters, from which they get their energy. Winds blowing in the same direction and at the same speed force air up from the ocean surface. As these winds flow outward above the storm, lower air is able to rise. Water vapor in this humid air changes from a gas to a liquid, forming the storm's clouds. This releases heat into the air, powering the storm further. Light winds outside the storm steer it and let it grow.

Many tropical cloud systems form each year during hurricane season. But only a few have the

This picture of the eye of a hurricane was taken by the *Apollo 7* spaceship in 1968.

perfect mix of conditions needed to become a hurricane.

Naming Hurricanes

The United States began using women's names to identify storms in 1953. In 1979 meteorologists began to alternate between male and female names for storms. Today the World Meteorological Organization names storms. Each year the first storm's name begins with an *A*, followed in alphabetical order by names beginning with the other letters of the alphabet. If a storm is particularly damaging or deadly, its name is permanently retired. Hurricane Sandy's name will likely never be used again.

Hurricane Anatomy

A hurricane's wind and clouds swirl around a central area called the eye. A hurricane's eye is cloudless and relatively calm. The eye is approximately 20 to 40 miles (32–64 km) across. Sometimes people think a hurricane is over when the eye passes because conditions become so calm. But the eye is only a pause before the storm strikes again.

The part of the storm called the eye wall encircles the eye. It is the most dangerous part of the hurricane. The eye wall contains dense clouds that produce violent winds.

Hurricanes also have rainbands. These are spiraling bands of thunderstorms. They develop 100 to 300 miles (161–483 km) from the hurricane's center.

How Sandy Became a Superstorm

Two days before making landfall in the United States, Sandy developed several unusual weather features. It began to resemble a large winter storm, similar to what people call a nor'easter. But Sandy still had a tropical core. It had become a hybrid of two dangerous types of storms. That is why people began to call it a superstorm. For the first time in US history, the government issued both hurricane and blizzard warnings for the same storm.

Sandy was also unusual because its wind gusts were strongest to the west of the eye. This was because Sandy was expected to join with another storm system growing to the west. Several other factors also blocked the hurricane from moving east. This is very unusual for storms over the Atlantic Ocean. These factors combined to turn Sandy directly toward the East Coast of the United States, home to tens of millions of people.

Sandy proved to be much larger than a typical hurricane. By Saturday, October 27, its winds extended 105 miles (169 km) from its center. Winds at tropical storm levels were recorded over a 520-mile (837-km)

The Perfect Storm

Computer models predicted Sandy would combine with two other weather systems. As a result, meteorologists compared Sandy to Hurricane Grace. That storm hit New England in November 1991. Grace was called the Perfect Storm. Hurricane Grace merged with two other storms. This combined storm system swirled to the southwest and caused high winds, rain, and a storm surge in New England. But Grace had lost much of its strength by the time it combined with the other two storms. And it did not make landfall after it combined with those storms.

area. The only recorded storm in the Atlantic Ocean larger than Sandy was Hurricane Olga in 2001. At one point, areas from the Mississippi River in the west all the way to the island of Bermuda in the east were experiencing the effects of Sandy at the same time.

Storm Surges

Storm surges are another danger caused by hurricanes. Storm surges are caused by spiraling winds pushing huge amounts of water toward shore. When a hurricane makes landfall, this water spills over the land. A storm surge floods everything in its path.

The amount of floodwater that comes ashore due to a storm surge depends on whether the tide is low or high at the time. For example, when a tide that is 2 feet (1 m) above sea level combines with a 10-foot (3-m) storm surge, the combined water is 12 feet (4 m) higher than sea level.

Scientists and officials were worried about Sandy's potential storm surge in New York and New Jersey. The NHC predicted a maximum storm surge

New York City prepared for the possibility of high storm surges and flooding caused by Superstorm Sandy by blocking off certain areas with sandbags.

of 11 feet (3 m) in Battery Park. This area sits on the coastline in New York City. They expected such a high storm surge because there would be a full moon the night Sandy was due to land. A full moon causes higher tides.

With storm surge and high winds on their minds, East Coast residents prepared for the worst.

EXPLORE ONLINE

Chapter Two explains the parts of a hurricane and how hurricanes form. It also explains storm surges. The Web site below also provides general information about hurricanes. As you know, every source is different. How is the information given in this Web site different from the information in this chapter? What information is the same? How do the two sources present information differently? What can you learn from this Web site?

All about Hurricanes
www.mycorelibrary.com/superstorm-sandy

CHAPTER THREE

PREPARING FOR SANDY

As Sandy approached the East Coast, officials prepared for a massive disaster. Sandy was about to hit the most populous area of the country. More than 8 million people live in New York City. Millions more live in New Jersey and other areas that were in Sandy's path.

A manager boards up a store's windows in Ocean City, Maryland, in preparation for Superstorm Sandy.

A large crowd gathered in North Wildwood, New Jersey, to listen to Governor Chris Christie discuss preparations for dealing with Superstorm Sandy.

The Government Warns the Public

President Barack Obama warned officials to take the storm seriously and prepare. New Jersey's governor, Chris Christie, also took the storm seriously. On October 28, he ordered residents of the state's barrier islands to evacuate. He also told people to listen to forecasters' warnings about Sandy.

On October 28 New York City mayor Michael Bloomberg ordered more than 370,000 people to evacuate. The city's schools closed on October 29. The city also ordered subways, buses, and trains to stop operating. Pilots stopped flying into New York City and surrounding areas.

From North Carolina to Connecticut, state and local governments asked residents in other coastal communities to leave their homes. Schools and public transportation closed in major cities such as Baltimore, Boston, and Washington DC.

The Presidential Election

While Sandy spun toward the East Coast, the 2012 US presidential election was only a week away. As a result, President Obama canceled several days of campaigning. Obama's Republican opponent, Mitt Romney, also stopped campaigning for several days. Campaign workers instead handed out storm supplies to those in need.

A power company official in Colchester, Vermont, checks a status board in preparation for Superstorm Sandy. East Coast officials warned residents to expect power outages.

Getting Ready for Sandy

Thousands of East Coast residents left their homes to find shelter. So many people decided to drive out of the area some gas stations ran out of fuel. But many people decided to stay in their homes. They ignored warnings they might not be safe.

Quite a few people decided to stay because of their experience with 2011's Hurricane Irene. Some people felt leaving their homes during that storm had been unnecessary. They did not want to make the same mistake again. They prepared by stocking up on essentials, such as bottled water, canned food, and flashlights. They also put sandbags outside their homes to prevent flooding. They boarded up windows to prevent the wind from breaking them. Some people bought power generators to use if they lost electricity.

After days of skirting the East Coast, Sandy sped up to 90 miles per hour (145 km/h). It then made a sharp turn to the

Frankenstorm

Meteorologist James Cisco gave Sandy the nickname Frankenstorm. One reason for this was because Sandy hit the East Coast close to Halloween. Frankenstein is the name of a famous monster people often dress as for Halloween. The monster was made up of many different parts. In a way, Superstorm Sandy was made up of different parts of storms.

Superstorm Sandy's Path

This is a map of the path taken by Superstorm Sandy through the Caribbean and along the East Coast of the United States. Several factors prevented Sandy from moving east over the Atlantic Ocean. It turned west instead, making landfall in New Jersey. How does seeing this map help you to more clearly understand the path Sandy took from its birthplace near Jamaica?

northwest. An hour before Sandy struck, it became

a post-tropical cyclone. Post-tropical cyclones are

storms that were once tropical in nature but now

get their energy from the contrasts between the

atmosphere's warm and cool air. This is different from hurricanes, which pull heat from the ocean.

On October 29, people on the East Coast braced for impact. The worst of the storm would hit later that evening.

CHAPTER FOUR

SUPERSTORM SANDY STRIKES

At 8:00 p.m. on Monday, October 29, Superstorm Sandy hit an area near Atlantic City, New Jersey. Its 80-mile-per-hour (129-km/h) winds destroyed buildings. Heavy rains and a strong storm surge followed. This caused massive flooding. High winds felled trees and downed power lines. More than 8 million people in 17 states were left without power.

Waves crash into Carolina Beach, North Carolina, as Superstorm Sandy approaches the East Coast.

Waves wash over the Jet Star roller coaster, which fell into the Atlantic Ocean in Seaside Heights, New Jersey, during Superstorm Sandy.

New Jersey

In New Jersey, Sandy tore boardwalks along beaches to pieces. It destroyed coastal amusement parks. Bridges leading to the barrier islands collapsed. A storm surge caused the Hackensack River to overflow. Floodwaters raced through small towns in Bergen County, near New York City. Within 30 minutes, Moonachie, a town of 2,700 people, was submerged.

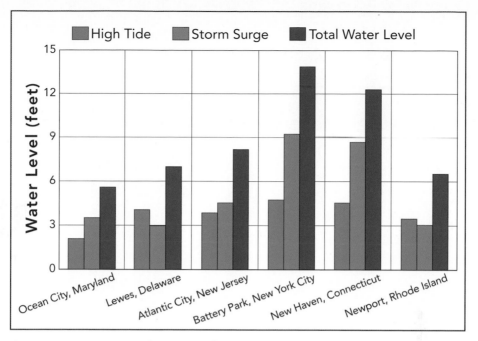

Superstorm Sandy's Peak Water Levels

This chart shows information about the storm surges created by Superstorm Sandy. How did water levels at Battery Park compare with other areas? What area had the highest storm surge? What area had the lowest? How did the tide play a factor in those water levels? How does seeing this chart help you understand storm surges?

New York City

After Sandy ripped through New Jersey, its howling winds hit New York City. Roads, subway tracks, and tunnels flooded. The peak water level in Battery Park reached almost 14 feet (4 m). This high storm surge surpassed the old Battery Park record of 10 feet (3 m) set by Hurricane Donna in 1960.

Soon lower Manhattan, part of New York City, found itself in darkness. The electricity company, Consolidated Edison, turned off power to 6,500 residents. The company did this to avoid further water damage. As the storm raged, the company cut off power to another 250,000 customers.

In Breezy Point, a beach community in the neighborhood of Queens, many homes caught fire just as Sandy landed. The raging storm kept firefighters from putting out the blazes as they moved from house to house. Sandy's winds intensified the fires.

Sandy Sinks Famous Ship

The HMS *Bounty* was a recreation of a famous British sailing ship from the 1700s. Filmmakers used the ship in several movies, including *Pirates of the Caribbean: Dead Man's Chest*. As Hurricane Sandy struck the ship off the coast of North Carolina on October 29, crewmembers scurried into lifeboats. The US Coast Guard used helicopters and rescue swimmers to save 14 of the ship's 16 sailors. Rescuers never found the ship's captain, Robin Walbridge.

The tiny beachfront community of Breezy Point in the New York City neighborhood of Queens was devastated by both floodwaters and fires that destroyed many homes.

Post-Tropical Blizzard

While Sandy brought rain and flooding to the East Coast, it also dumped snow on states farther west. Seven states dealt with the massive snowstorm created by Sandy. The mountains of West Virginia and Maryland received the most snow. Two to three feet (0.5–1 m) of snow fell in those areas. The dense snow caused tree branches to snap, power lines to fall, and the roofs of buildings to collapse. Authorities had to close some interstate highways because they were too dangerous for travelers.

More than 100 houses burned to the ground.

After the storm battered New Jersey and New York, it headed into Pennsylvania. On October 31 Sandy finally weakened over the Great Lakes, ending its path of destruction.

Writing student Jennifer Fitzgerald wrote a poem about Hurricane Sandy called "I Cannot Show You the Streets under the Rubble":

The sun teased through the clouds; I watched it land
on the debris, illuminating soaked sheetrock, support
*   beams,*
a child's stuffed panda. You can't discern what came from
the ocean, what the ocean tore out. Say it, Storm Surge,

alliteration masks the weight of 20 foot waves pulling
themselves down on top of you. . . .

Source: Jennifer Fitzgerald. "MFA student captures Hurricane Sandy through poetry, on PBS." Lesley University. Lesley University, November 26, 2012. Web. Accessed February 17, 2013.

What's the Big Idea?

Take a close look at Jennifer Fitzgerald's poem. What is her main point? What language does she use to support her point? Write a few sentences showing how Fitzgerald uses two or three details to support her main point.

SANDY'S AFTERMATH

Superstorm Sandy wreaked havoc on the East Coast. The storm killed at least 125 Americans. On October 30 President Obama declared ten states major disaster areas. Government officials estimated the storm caused approximately $62 billion in damages.

Sandy was the second most expensive storm in US history. The most costly was Hurricane Katrina. This

Superstorm Sandy destroyed hundreds of homes in New Jersey's coastal areas.

storm rampaged through New Orleans, Louisiana, in 2005.

Dealing with the Storm's Aftermath

Thousands of people were left homeless by Sandy. Others had no power for weeks. These conditions became especially dangerous when temperatures approached freezing. To make matters worse, the same areas affected by Sandy had to deal with a nor'easter on November 7. Once again, East Coast residents endured cold temperatures, strong winds, rain, and snow.

Plans for the Future

As people picked up the pieces of their lives after Sandy, talk turned to protecting coastal cities from the next big storm. In New York, Governor Andrew Cuomo stressed the need for larger, movable seawalls. Seawalls protect an area from flooding. Manhattan's seawalls are only four to five feet (1–2 m) above sea level. Sandy's storm surge had no problem flowing over them.

Mayor Bloomberg disagreed with strengthening seawalls. He said seawalls would be too expensive, difficult to build, and unreliable. He wanted New York City to take a more natural approach. For example, he agreed with experts who said the city could create wetlands and marshes where water and land meet. These natural habitats would soak up water and reduce the impact of strong storm surges. Another idea was to make streets out of porous

Volunteers Lend a Hand

Charity organizations such as the American Red Cross helped those hurt by Sandy. By November 27, the organization had provided shelter to more than 14,400 people. The charity handed out more than 7.4 million meals. Several other organizations contributed to hurricane relief efforts as well. The Disney/ABC Television Group held a Day of Giving fundraiser, raising $17 million. The Concert for Sandy Relief brought together many popular musical performers to earn money to help Sandy's victims.

Superstorm Sandy's powerful storm surges flooded many of New York City's deep subway tunnels.

concrete. This would allow water to soak through to the ground below, reducing flooding.

Whatever choices officials make, East Coast residents know their region will always be at risk for another hurricane. They are working with government officials to make changes to their communities. Just as when Sandy hit, Americans will always work together to clean up and recover from the damage of large, dangerous weather events.

In his speech after Superstorm Sandy, President Barack Obama acknowledged the difficulties many people were experiencing and spoke of the American spirit:

> *I think all of us obviously have been shocked by the force of Mother Nature as we watch it on television. At the same time, we've also seen nurses at NYU Hospital carrying fragile newborns to safety. We've seen incredibly brave firefighters in Queens, waist-deep in water, battling infernos and rescuing people in boats. . . .*
>
> *This is a tough time for a lot of people—millions of folks all across the Eastern Seaboard. But America is tougher, and we're tougher because we pull together. We leave nobody behind. We make sure that we respond as a nation and remind ourselves that whenever an American is in need, all of us stand together to make sure that we're providing the help that's necessary.*

Source: Barack Obama. "Transcript: Obama's remarks about Hurricane Sandy at the Red Cross today." Chicago Sun-Times. Sun-Times Media, October 30, 2012. Web. Accessed March 5, 2013

Back It Up

In this speech, President Obama uses evidence to support a point. Write a paragraph describing the point he is making. Then write down two or three pieces of evidence he uses to make his point.

IMPORTANT DATES 2012

Oct. 22

The National Hurricane Center names Sandy as the eighteenth tropical storm of 2012.

Oct. 24

Sandy becomes a hurricane and makes landfall in Jamaica.

Oct. 24

Violent storms caused by Hurricane Sandy strike Haiti.

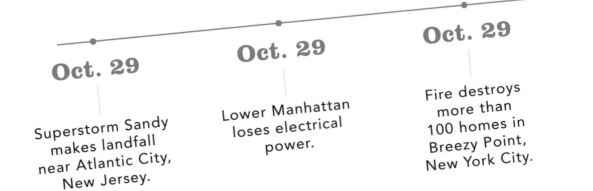

Oct. 29

Superstorm Sandy makes landfall near Atlantic City, New Jersey.

Oct. 29

Lower Manhattan loses electrical power.

Oct. 29

Fire destroys more than 100 homes in Breezy Point, New York City.

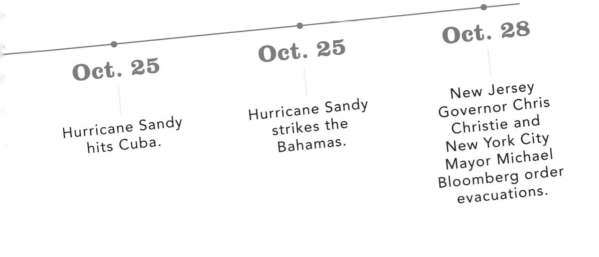

Oct. 25

Hurricane Sandy hits Cuba.

Oct. 25

Hurricane Sandy strikes the Bahamas.

Oct. 28

New Jersey Governor Chris Christie and New York City Mayor Michael Bloomberg order evacuations.

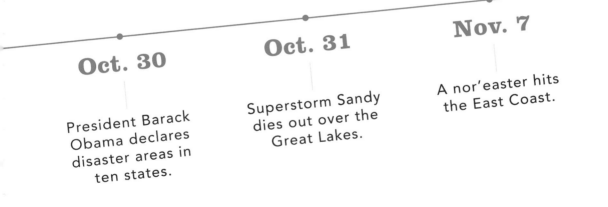

Oct. 30

President Barack Obama declares disaster areas in ten states.

Oct. 31

Superstorm Sandy dies out over the Great Lakes.

Nov. 7

A nor'easter hits the East Coast.

STOP AND THINK

Say What?

Studying hurricanes can mean learning many new words. Find five words in this book you have never read before. Use a dictionary to find their meaning. Write the meanings in your own words, and use each word in a sentence.

Take a Stand

Chapter Five discusses ways New York City might protect itself from future hurricanes. Some people feel the city's seawall should be strengthened. Others think the city should use a more natural approach. What do you think is the best plan? Write a short essay explaining your opinion. Make sure to give reasons for your opinion and details supporting those reasons.

You Are There

This book discusses how people prepared for Hurricane Sandy. Imagine you live in a coastal New Jersey community. How would you and your family prepare for the storm? What supplies would you need? What would you do to keep safe?

Why Do I Care?

This book describes Hurricane Sandy's destructive path. Can you find any similarities between your life and the people who lived through the hurricane? Have you ever experienced a dangerous weather event, such as a thunderstorm, blizzard, or tornado? How did this affect your life?

GLOSSARY

eye
the center of a hurricane, which is relatively calm

eye wall
the region surrounding the eye of a hurricane, which usually contains dense clouds and the storm's strongest winds and heaviest rainfall

nor'easter
a strong storm along the East Coast of the United States, usually in winter

post-tropical cyclone
a storm that has transitioned from being tropical in nature to getting its energy from the contrasts between the atmosphere's warm and cool air

rainbands
areas that consist of spiraling thunderstorms surrounding a hurricane

storm surge
an abnormal rise in water driven by high winds

tropical cyclone
the general name for storms like hurricanes, typhoons, and cyclones, all of which originate in the tropics

tropical depression
rotating winds that form in the tropics

tropical storm
a rotating storm system that forms in the tropics and has winds of 39 to 73 miles per hour (63–117 km/h)

LEARN MORE

Books

Gibbons, Gail. *Hurricanes!* New York: Holiday House, 2010.

Hojem, Benjamin. *Hurricanes: Weathering the Storm.* New York: Grosset & Dunlap, 2010.

Simon, Seymour. *Hurricanes.* New York: HarperCollins, 2007.

Web Links

To learn more about Superstorm Sandy, visit ABDO Publishing Company online at **www.abdopublishing.com**. Web sites about Superstorm Sandy are featured on our Book Links page. These links are routinely monitored and updated to provide the most current information available.

Visit **www.mycorelibrary.com** for free additional tools for teachers and students.

INDEX

ABOUT THE AUTHOR

Rachel Bailey grew up in a small Kansas town near Kansas City. As a child, she enjoyed reading, bicycling, and taking nature walks. Rachel is a former teacher. She now writes children's magazine articles and educational curriculum for teachers.